Abraham

Olwyn Harris

Reflections on a man
who was known as the friend of God

Suitable for Individual and Group Discussion

Copyright © Olwyn Harris 2025

ISBN   Softcover   978-1-923021-32-7
       eBook   978-1-923021-33-4

All rights reserved. No part of this book may be reproduced or transmitted in any form or by any means, electronic, or mechanical, including photocopying, recording or by any information storage and retrieval system without the permission in writing by the copyright owner.
Unless otherwise stated Scriptures quoted here are from the King James Version (Authorised version). First published in 1611. Quoted from the KJV Classic Reference Bible, copyright 1983 by the Zondervan Corporation.

Published by: Reading Stones Publishing
Helen Brown & Wendy Wood
Woodwendy1982.wixsite.com/readingstones
Cover Design: Olwyn Harris. Some of the cover elements were created using AI Technology.

For more copies contact the publisher at:

Glenburnie
212 Glenburnie Road
ROB ROY NSW 2360
Mobile: 0422 577 663
Email: Readingstonespublishing@gmail.com

Acknowledgement:

My heartfelt appreciation to Pastor Dawn Peel, emeritus, who has held a role as part of the credentialing of pastors within the ACC church. Thank you for your willingness to cast your theological eye over these chapters.

Table of Contents

Abraham

Table of Contents	5
Introduction	7
The Call of Friendship	9
Abram – The Peacemaker	23
Abram – The Just	41
Abraham – The Obedient	54
Abraham - The Merciful	68
Abraham – The Faithful	83
Endnotes	99

Introduction

Taking time to reflect on the stories in the Bible, is something that we are encouraged to do in our walk with Jesus. I don't know anyone who would suggest this is not an important aspect of being a disciple of Jesus. Yet I have noticed, over and over, there is a widespread illiteracy regarding the stories in the Bible which I grew up with. I've also noticed that this unfamiliarity is not restricted to new Christians. I suspect we are more comfortable with the popular narratives on our TV streaming service, than the ones in our Bible.

The Holy Spirit, in his wisdom, has chosen the platform of storytelling as one way to communicate our spiritual relationship him, packed with wisdom, truth, morality, and values. It is not the only way God speaks to us, yet so much practical wisdom can be distilled from these narratives. Our challenge is how to access these stories in a way that allows them to be understandable in a world that is so far removed from the times when these accounts occurred. This series on *Reflections in the Bible* is not intended to be an exercise in theological exegesis, rather to create an opportunity to explore some of these stories. It is an invitation to go on a journey of reflection around what is described. What can we distil from these life-stories that makes sense for us today? Some of these narratives may be familiar. Some of them may be forgotten. Some of them are hard to understand. This is an opportunity to take time to slow down, invite the Holy Spirit to whisper his insight as we explore some of the stories he has preserved for us.

This book is intended to be a reflective space to use alongside your Bible. Sometimes, even the act of opening the pages of our Bible can be a challenge. So, open up! Don't skip over the suggested passages marked as "Bible Readings". The scriptures tagged as "Bible Reference" are intended to bookmark passages, if you want to check them. Take hold of the opportunity to read or revisit God's Word. You are invited to use these pages as a place to scribble in margins; explore your own questions; and use reflective prompts to go a little deeper. My prayer is that it will be a springboard to explore the incredible love story of God, his great good news of redemption and His grace will draw you closer to who He is as our Good Father. I trust it moves each of us to appreciate more about our relationship with God, ourselves and life in community.

1.
The Call of Friendship

Sometimes, the way we think about God, glorified and seated in heavenly places, although this is true, can make God and our relationship with Jesus feel inaccessible. Other worldly. Out of reach. Yet Jesus said something quite remarkable to his disciples during the Last Supper: He said to them "You're my friends!"

Bible Reading
John 15:12-17

We are invited into Friendship - Not a workforce

Jesus says, "I have chosen you, called you... not to be my workforce, but to be my friends."

> Not students of a Rabbi... friends...
> Not servants of a master... friends...
> Not on duty as a staff... friends...

Friends, hanging out, enjoying being together; on the same page working together; sharing our stuff with each other... personal and private stuff.

What is it like to think that Jesus wants me to be his friend?

Jesus said this to his disciples as he was leaving... not while they were walking around together, doing life together. He is flipping the idea of discipleship on its head. Disciples were there to serve their rabbi. They were there to learn how to think, to work, to operate... to function. But Jesus tells them that is an incomplete perspective. Yes, there is work, and instructions, and things that are needed to be accomplished... but it happens from a place of friendship... not servitude.

So, what does it look like... to be a friend of God? A friend of Jesus... A friend of the Holy Spirit?

In my circle of friendships, what do my healthiest friendships look like?

What ways could I enrich my friendship with God?

The prophet Micah has identified what God requires of his people...

Bible Reading
Micah 6:8
If you can read this again in The Message, or another contemporary translation.

What do you notice about what God desires of his people?

How could I do these things better?

Walk alongside...

This is what God calls us to do... not as servants on duty... but as his friends... walking along-side him through life. Including God in the strong times... and the challenging times... and the weak times... This is what God is looking for... regardless of what is going on... justice, mercy and a humble walk that doesn't take ourselves too seriously... but takes God seriously.

The Witness of Scripture

One way to explore this idea is to go to the stories in our Bible where we meet people who were able to do this well. And there is someone, who is known in scripture, as 'the friend of God': As King Jehoshaphat is praying... he identifies one who is friend of God

Bible Reference
2 Chronicles 20:7

Isaiah the prophet speaks this...

Bible Reference
Isaiah 41:8

And James in the New Testament says this:

Bible Reference
James 2:23

I do look for the principle of two or three witnesses in scripture. It is a principle that Moses writes about in Deuteronomy. Two or three witnesses were a legal requirement when "establishing a matter".

Bible Reference
Deuteronomy 19:15

This is a spiritual principle that can be applied... two or three witnesses verifies the accuracy of a matter; it offers a point of emphasis. Here we find three witnesses in scripture that Abraham was this guy. He was a friend of God's. What God was looking for in a friend – Abraham was that person. He nailed it.

So rather than dive straight in and analyse the four factors and three dot-points that can identify what friend of God needs to be... let's walk alongside Abraham for a bit and see if we can identify those qualities that made him famous as a friend of God. We are introduced to Abraham in the Book of Genesis

Bible Reading
Genesis 11:27-31

Some Background: Ancient times & culture...
I think it is important to remember, when considering the life of Abraham – or Abram, which was his birth name... is that he lived in ancient times. Very ancient times. The ancient story of Job is said to be the oldest text in our scripture, and it is likely that Abram lived around the same time. We can't put Abram into the Roman culture of the New Testament and definitely not into our contemporary western culture and make sense of it.

The period of Abram's life is the era that comes after the flood of Noah. We are given a direct genealogy from Noah to Abram. According to the dates and long lives people lived, we can calculate that one of the sons of Noah, Shem, was still alive during Abram's life. We are not talking thousands of years post flood when these events happened... but only hundreds of years. For some people alive at that time... this was still living memory. People groups and tribes are still being established.

Families are forming their own cultures and identities, with their own tribal kings.

Abram challenged the cultural status quo

In this era, there were some people who understood and worshiped the one true creator God... particularly the families descended from Shem – one of the sons of Noah. People like Job, worshiped the One True God, faithfully.

But for many people... their culture involved the worship of other gods, and the very evil that God had addressed with the Great Flood has been re-established. They worshipped idols that they have made with their own hands. Creations of their own imagination. The god Molech was one of the deities worshiped at this time. Archaeological excavations[i] have discovered hundreds of ancient urns containing the charred bones of children, that were offered as sacrificial gifts to the god Molech. That is particularly significant when it comes to Abram's story.

This was the culture of Abram's day. The religious worship of idols is what his family was involved in... devotedly. There is an Ancient Hebrew book, called the "Book of Jasher", that is referred to a couple of times in the Old Testament[ii], but it has not been included in our Bible. So, although it is not designated as Holy Scripture, it is useful for exploring background and context.

The Book of Jasher gives us more information about Abram and his family. It tells us that Abran's father Terah, was an idol maker... and he was an influential man because of his profession. But Abram began to question and challenge the religious status quo. The idea of worshiping things made with your own hands made no sense to him.

"...idols of wood and stone which can neither eat, smell, hear nor speak, who have mouths without speech, eyes without sight, ears without hearing, hands without feeling, and legs which cannot move"
(Book of Jasher 11:32)

Acted on his convictions
This book includes a story that one day, Abram went into the shrine where lots of these idols were kept and smashed them up with a hatchet. And as a final symbolic gesture, he placed the hatchet in the arms of the largest idol, the only one that he left standing.

Are there idols that I need to smash?

Abram's father, Terah, was furious... and he accosted him. Abram said something like... "Gee... it must have been the big idol that did all the damage, because he's holding the hatchet! Perhaps he was jealous for the offerings that were given to the others."

Terah is not fooled. He said to Abram, something to the effect of, "Well that's obviously a lie! They are just made of stone and wood. They can't do what you say. I know because I made them myself."

Exactly! Why would you worship and defend something that has no power to do anything, much less deliver you?

In what ways do I just accept the cultural status quo around me?

How could I look at this in a way, so that I see what God sees?

Where would it be appropriate for me to challenge the status quo, and do my life differently?

According to the Book of Jasher, Terah was so angry with Abram, that he brought Abram before their king and he was put on trial for religious abuses. He was sentenced to be executed by fire because he refused to be moved from his convictions, and the story goes that God saved him, in an experience similar to Shadrach, Meshach and Abednego. Abram escaped and went into hiding. When Terah found him, he agreed that they would all leave the country, because there was still a contract out on Abram's head because of the disrespect he showed these local deities.

So, Terah's whole family left Chaldea to move to Canaan, but they didn't get as far as Canaan. About halfway along the journey, they settled in Haran. And then, it is after Terah died, that we pick up the story in Genesis 12.

Bible Reading
Genesis 12:1-7

God Spoke...
This is something that we hardly even notice when we read the story: "The Lord said to Abram..." We are used to this... God speaking to his people. We take it for granted. But right here we have such a strong contrast to the gods of his father's shrines. This is a God who spoke! The true God who communicated... who was alive! This is a God who wanted to engage and be part of his life... personally... not generically.

There is also another stark contrast to the experience of the worshippers of the gods of his father. Rather than a god who takes and takes and takes... this God is a God who blesses! This is a God who personally called Abram... with the expressed purpose to bless him and his family. And to bless others through him. Actually, more than that... to bless all the people of the world through him.

Abram set out
And so, when God spoke... Abram set out. This was the God who was worth pulling up stakes for.

At the time when my husband and I had a conviction that God was asking us to relocate to North Queensland, I remember certain friends being quite concerned that we were being irrational.
We sold our house... a family home that we had just built... to live in a donga the size of a single garage, with 3 teenagers. We resigned our jobs... that were our dream jobs... for jobs that were less ideal and lived with the challenges of periods of unemployment.

But what I noticed about that time, was that it was not hard, because there was an internal "heart-burn" on the inside, that God was all over what was happening for us.

There was another reality that was part of the equation for me... probably not so much for my husband. It was the idea that to sell the house was important because I didn't trust myself not to bail, if and when things got hard. Obedience to the conviction of God's leading was important to me... and I figured, that if I bombed the bridges behind me, there would be no going back.

The reality is that if we had a brand new 5-bedroom house waiting for us down South... we may have left that appointment prematurely. We felt God was repositioning us, and we wanted to be part of what he was doing, in us and through us.

Abram had discovered the Alive God who was worth his investment of everything he had. Abram had a good life in Haran. He had prospered there... but the blessing God had for Abram was not just for good... it was for *great*. A great nation.

Yet a great life... came at a cost. The cost was to follow this great God... and to do it his way... not Abram's way. And God says that His way. was to leave everything behind.

>Leave his father's house... leave the way of his ancestors...
>Leave his old style of worship...
>Leave his idols
>Leave his accumulated stuff...
>Leave his old life... and start completely new.

Are there things I need to courageously leave behind so God can do something new in my life?

For us in Australia, leaving like that, is probably not so shocking. Families in our culture are nuclear by nature. Extended family is often fairly loose compared to other cultures where extended family is valued and esteemed and honoured. In Australia... moving locations and large distances is not unusual. In the 2016 census 43% of Australians had changed addresses from the previous census, that's just under half the entire population. That year, 77 000 people moved to Qld. 66 000 Queenslanders left Queensland.

Unlike our indigenous counterparts, generally we are not a people who have strong connections to place. It is not usual to stay in one place for a lifetime... much less for multiple generations. It is unusual to have family homes that are passed down.

Since we were married, we have lived in 13 different places... some of those, interstate.

I've wondered why we don't hear about the God of Terah, Abraham, Isaac and Jacob, because this era was marked as a culture of generations... and after all we have a reliable record of whose Abram's father was. And the answer is here. God is starting something new. To do that... Abram needs to courageously leave behind the house of his father. Abram needed to step outside what is comfortable, for the next part of his story.

Abram is being designated as the patriarch, the head of his house...not his father house.

    Abram doesn't hesitate
    He doesn't argue
    He doesn't resist
    He doesn't settle

He sets out... on this grand adventure. Terah was already on the way to Canaan when they left the land of the Chaldeans, but he had settled in

Haran. This time, Abram is going to the place that God will show him, not designated by his father.

The destination is not exact... he doesn't really know where he is going... but God will show him. It requires staying close to God as his GPS – his 'global positioning system'. Or perhaps that is more correctly... his 'God's Positioning System'. It requires listening, and being guided, and being guide-able... according to God's plans. Doing it together. Staying close... like a friend.

Am I tuned into God's GPS, his positioning for those plans he has for me?

Worshiped God

When Abram arrives at Shechem, God speaks again. This is the area in Samaria, between the foothills of Mt Ebal and Mt Gerizum. During Jesus' ministry, this is where Jesus stopped to rest at Jacob's well and he spoke with the woman at the well. Abram stopped there... generations before... to worship God and offer sacrifices, and God speaks to him.

God says to Abram: "This is the land I will give your offspring..."
This is the promise I have for you. It is a two-part promise:
> A homeland... a footprint... a place... a heritage... a legacy.
> And then the second part of the promise was offspring.

Even at 75 years of age, Abram has no children. But the promise is there. Abram built an altar to the Lord. He acknowledged God's promise. He honoured God with sacrifices and worship. He worshiped and loved God in the way that he knew: with sacrifices and offerings. And it says God appeared to him there. God met him.Manifested. Face to face... like a friend.

Final Thoughts...
Abram is identified as a Friend of God. But his life didn't start that way. His family manufactured, worshiped and honoured handmade idols. Yet, as Abram challenges the things he sees around him, he meets the One True God.
    The God who appears to him
    The God who meets with him
    The God who speaks with him
    The God who blesses generously, rather than just takes and takes.
As Abram invests in this relationship, this friendship with God, he leaves behind his old life and starts a new adventure with God.

I remember getting a phone call from a lady I knew from church.
She wanted to do coffee. I had done a short work contract for her before and I knew in my spirit, that she wanted to offer me a job.
The problem was that I had a job. At this point, I had been at my job for nine months. It had been a huge learning curve, and I had just got to the point where I felt comfortable my role, and on top of managing my workload. I had even recently sat at my computer and thanked God for getting me through. "This is good God. Thank you. I am happy now and can keep going here indefinitely."
And then this lady offered me a job. Hmm...
I didn't want her job offer... so over coffee... I said, "Thanks, but no thanks..."
But afterwards I felt convicted that I should at least explore the opportunity and know what I was saying "no" to. As I read the Position Description, the role was much more than I had initially thought. It was plugging into my nursing background, rehabilitation and return to work

plans. This was something I had wanted to do for a long time. I still didn't really want to resign where I was, but this felt like God was opening a door for me.

When I rang her and said I would take the position, she was surprised. She said, "I didn't expect you to say yes." When I asked her about that, she said, "You said you were happy where you are, and I know you are loyal; I couldn't see you moving..."

Well... I thought... it was the right thing to do. What I find remarkable about this was that a short time later, barely a couple of months, maybe 6 or 8 weeks, the business where I had been working was sold. It was absorbed into another organisation. The whole thing was shut down and my old job, no longer existed. I am grateful I listened to the internal God positioning system and that I moved... when he said to move. I haven't always done that, but in this situation, I am grateful that I did.

God is for us. He wants to be our friend. He wants us to trust him. He doesn't ask things of us, just to make our life uncomfortable, but sometimes it does mean moving out of the comfort of what is familiar towards something new. So, he can bless us, and so that we can be a conduit of blessing to others as well.

Abram was able to do that. His call was not just to a location, but to walk in friendship with God along the journey of his life. That involved challenging some things in his background. It meant stepping out and making changes. It meant worshiping only God and not taking on the culture of the people around him, even when that culture was embraced by the family he grew up with. Perhaps these are some of the qualities that makes Abram a friend of God.

Prayer:
Father God, it is a privilege to know that you have called up your friends. Thank you that you don't make it a mystery of what that looks like, but there is actually a very clear understanding of what you require as we walk alongside you. God, we pray that you would help us to love sincerely, to act justly, and to walk humbly, and take you seriously because you are the most important in our lives.
In Jesus Name, Amen.

2.

Abram – The Peacemaker

Where we have been...

The ideas that Jesus called his disciples "friends" have launched us looking into the life of Abraham... or Abram, as his birth name is, so that we can see what it looks like to be a friend of God. Abraham is good place to explore these ideas because he is a man who is famously known as a "friend of God".

Abram encounters a living God who spoke... not like the idols of his father. He was called to go to a new place, to be a man who would be the conduit of blessing for all his descendants, and from there to all the people of the earth. Yet almost straight away we are given a story about Abram that seems a little off... a little bit dodgy.

Bible Reading
Genesis 12:10-20

Getting off-track

In the land of promise, things get tough. Famine and sparsity do not seem like much of a blessing and Abram's response is to leave. Escape. Survive. It is not an uncommon perspective that by going to Egypt, Abram was abandoning the place of promise and hardship causes him to be derailed from God's plan. That's a negative take on what he did.

Am I inclined to think that the choices I have made, where I have got off track, will forever ruin the possibility of restoration?

But there is also the opposite idea, that Egypt becomes a place of refuge. A refuge is a place of safety, to hold and protect during a time of hardship. Egypt had constant water... the River Nile. We see Egypt as a place of refuge in other stories in the Bible.

Joseph was sent to Egypt ahead of Jacob's family so they would be rescued from a vast famine

Bible Reference
Genesis 50:20

Mary, the mother of Jesus, and her husband Joseph escaped to Egypt with Jesus as a young child to avoid the massacre decreed by King Herod.

Bible Reference
Matthew 2:13-15

Regardless of whether or not Abram should have stayed in land of promise, or what the strongest rationale was to move him on for a season, we can acknowledge that life can throw at us big challenges that can cause us to detour.

But things can get really messy when we meet those challenges by trying to blend in so that we are not noticed or don't stand out. It results in stepping outside the parameters of God's best life for us. I don't think it as important as to why Abram left the place of promise to go to Egypt, but rather the way he managed his life when he did leave is significant.

Protects himself
Remember, we said that Abram lived in very ancient times. Ancient times that were violent and self-seeking. The pattern is that most powerful people win; and the least powerful loose. Abram is in Egypt

on a mission of self-preservation. This was the reason he left Canaan... to survive.

What is surprising is that Abram identifies his greatest vulnerability at this time, is his wife. Sarai is beautiful. Stunning. Miss Universe stunning. The kind of stunning that turns heads. The kind of beauty that Kings deserve and will take, at the cost of a man's life. Destroying others, so you can get the girl... this is not a new plot line. This is as old as Abraham. And he knew this.

Does it bother you that Sarai is in her seventies at this time? Does this make the story unrealistic and unbelievable?

Well, if we are looking at this account through a 21st century lens, that is a problem. I've never seen a 70-year-old win a beauty pageant not matter what skin care products they use. But keep in mind: Ancient story... Ancient times.

Pre and post flood, people lived long lives... very long lives. Terah lived to 215. Abraham lived to be 175. If this is your life expectancy, then 70 years old is your prime. You're not even middle aged yet, and you probably still to peak. Sarai is not seventy, with a walking frame. She is in her flush of femininity, very beautiful.

Abram's plan to manage this, is to go with the part-truth, the half-lie, to protect himself, to blend in. Sarai was his half-sister – the daughter of Terah, but not from his mother. To us, this is incest... back then, in these ancient times, there were no rules or taboos about which singles you could marry.

So, Abram and Sarai were married legitimately, but Abram fears for his life, and only tells the Egyptians, "She's, my sister." It seems he was comfortable to perpetuate this half-lie, to blend in, and to have his wife taken into Pharoah's harem at the palace court.

One of the things that I dealt with pedantically with my kids as they were growing was the way we talk. Manners the rituals of 'please' and 'thank-you'. Not swearing for the sake of it. I spent a lot of time saying to my kids, "You are an intelligent person, with a strong vocabulary... choose a different word."
But when I went back to work after being a stay-at-home mother, I didn't have control over what happened in the workplace. And the thing that hit me hardest... was the talk. Their speech shocked me.
I remember coming away from my first tour of the factory floor, absolutely stunned. I felt nauseous. I literally wanted to vomit from all the vile filth that constantly poured from the workers' mouths. They were not bad workers or bad people. But their language! As I was walking up to the Admin block from the factory... feeling sick, I said to God, "I don't think I can do this. That is terrible. I don't want to that to become my normal. You are going to have to help me with this... because I don't think I can."
And the Holy Spirit said to me...
"That is their dialect. You can't expect them to speak Kingdom, because they don't belong to the Kingdom."
That helped. I could not expect others to speak a dialect they were never taught or had the resources to learn.

But it was not my dialect either. I didn't have to make it my native tongue. It wasn't. But it also released me to consider that if I needed to communicate and translate so they could understand. I could use their dialect, but intentionally, with a purpose, not becoming and blending and merging.... like a chameleon... until I sound like they sound.

I could legitimately hold to a different dialect, without judging their talk, because I was resourced from a different kingdom with a different dialect.

Abram faces the same choice that we are constantly faced with: How would he interact with the people around him? Would he blend in? Or would he make different choices?

Even though this is Abram... a man called by God, and given a promise of a great future, the way he chooses to blend in in Egypt is not honourable behaviour. We know this because God moves to correct it. I appreciate this about our scriptures. Mistakes are not whitewashed. Trips and falls are not justified. They happened, they are recorded, so we can see how God will not abandon us if, and when, we do the same. If we mess up, if we get off track, if circumstances detour us, God will redirect us. God will bring us back to himself, back to a place of friendship. God always leaves that door open. Just like the metaphor of the GPS, there will be a redirection to get us back towards the heart of God.

Perpetrated harm on others

I can appreciate the fear, and the anxiety, and the bunkering down in self-preservation, but it is also worth noting, that the decisions that we make, always impact others. We are never silos, just doing something that only affects ourselves. There are ripples and ripples and ripples. And these ripples did not just involve Abram and Sarai.

Actually, for Abram, it seems like his plan is working. He does well financially in Egypt. He increases his holdings in a season of famine. Success during this time, like today I guess, was measured by your inventory. Abram, who had left everything, now has inventory that is starting to increase to the point of impressive:

Bible Reference
Genesis 12:16

Now Abram is looking like a man with impressive inventory and with that comes significant influence. But acquiring stuff is not the goal – this is the mindset of a grabber not a giver. God is a generous God who calls us to be conduits of blessing, not hoarders of blessing.

Psalm 119 says this as a prayer:

Bible Reference
Psalm 119:36

The word translated "testimony" or "statutes" is also translated "witness". Witness... Witness to what?
Well... we witness an event... or a story... an account... an encounter... relationship.

This is not just about loving the Law of God – what is defined as right or wrong, but it is an invitation to be drawn towards those things that bear witness and pull us closer to God, rather than those things that will draw us away from him. God desires us to be people who will choose what will pull us closer to him and not toward selfish gain.

Yet here we see Abram, is chasing after the selfish gain, and his choice had consequences. I am a little bemused that the consequences of Abram's actions fall directly in Pharoah's court. Pharoah and his household come down with serious illness. Our Bible doesn't say how they work out that Sarai is the reason for this sudden inundation of sickness, but Josephus records that Pharoah consulted his pagan priests. They join the dots that it is on account of Sarai, who is the wife of the 'foreigner' Abram, that this trouble has broken out.

God redirects to prosper

Pharoah calls for Abram and restores Sarai to him. Then they are kicked out of Egypt. So, Abram leaves, and he leaves with inventory. Lots of inventory. And it is easy to think that God blessed Abram with prosperity. Stuff. Lots of stuff, and in some way that justifies the betrayal, and the deception, and the lies. But this is a very human lens, and a selfish, self-promoting definition of blessing. God's blessing is not really about stuff. In Genesis 15 God speaks to Abram…

Bible Reference
Genesis 15:1

Yes, God is a God who provides… and we will discover that Abram has a special revelation of God as Jehovah Jireh: The God who provides. But even before that, God tells Abram that he need not fear. God is blessing him with peace – no need to be afraid.

God is blessing him with protection – God is his shield.

God is blessing him with his presence – "I AM your very great reward".

How I define blessing? Is it about accumulating stuff and inventory?

This blessing is mostly about God's presence in his life, rich relationship... and strong friendship... togetherness. That is where the "very great" blessing is.

Abram, who in effect betrayed his marriage, is redirected back towards God. God redirects Abram to bring him back to himself, for blessing.
>Blessing... in relationship...
>Blessing... to be generous...
>Blessing... to pass on to others

And we find that Abram does come back around and gets back on track. He is learning about this principle of being a conduit of blessing to others, and the application of this principle starts at home.

Bible Reading
Genesis 13:1-13

Returns to the promise

It took a while... he went from place to place... but Abram did arrive back to the place of promise. The drought has broken. He returns to the place of promise and Abram built an altar there. While he was there, we notice something that is a little bit different to his relationship with God to this point.

Abram called on the name of the Lord. This is a change. Before... God spoke to Abram. God made contact first. God said this and Abram responded. But now, Abram called on God; Abram initiated the conversation. He called on the name of the Lord – Jehovah: The Self-Existent One or Eternal God. Abram didn't wait but reached out to the eternal creator God.

And it doesn't say what Abram spoke about exactly, but we notice he is back in the place of promise. He is back thinking about the things of God.

Back worshiping and praising and praying, realigning with his relationship with God. Doing things God's way, rather than Abram's way.

Recognises the challenge

However, with the accumulation of stuff, comes some serious strife in the camp. A Lot of strife... so to speak! When you have two people, with large capacities, staying in one space, the tendency is to try to develop a hierarchy: one up and one down. I don't actually think that separation was only way to manage this situation. It is not like they have to make things stretch to go around. This region was looking like the Garden of Eden... the lush Delta of the Nile. There were enough resources, but the people involved couldn't work together on this.

Equality and partnership is not something that they understood or could manage. They are in danger here of an out-and-out war. Lot's camp is fighting with Abram's camp. Abram's men are quarrelling with Lot's men. They are getting territorial, angry, possessive, vindictive.

Abram is the head of this household. Tribal chief. He is like a father to Lot, the son of his dead brother. According to Josephus, Lot is also Sarai's brother. It would have been culturally acceptable for Abram to pull rank. To enforce his position and protect the position of his stuff. He could have demanded his status be upheld. He could have...

We have already seen that Abram has no other family. No son, but he has adopted his nephew Lot as his own family. Lot has gone everywhere with him... even to Egypt. This is normal in extended families; it is to be expected.

Some have noted that God asked Abram to leave behind his father's household.

Bible Reference
Genesis 12:1

Lot was of Terah's household, so technically Abram should have left Lot behind. Perhaps if Abram had really listened to God, Lot would not be here, fighting with him in a territorial dog fight over land, and water, and pasture. Perhaps God's directive was not about being mean and isolating Abram from his family, but forestalling problems into the future... this kind of problem. Perhaps it was intended as a protection, but now Abram was required to deal with the fall out. Because they have really fallen out.

I feel a little sad that it was the accumulation of stuff that separated these two. The amount of stuff that they both had, made this relationship no longer sustainable. Stuff got in the way of relationship.

When has stuff got in the way of me getting along with others?

They couldn't work out how solve this problem of sharing abundant resources together. Neither of them are on the bread-line. Both of them have plenty... more than plenty. But rather than become enemies Abram decides they should separate.

We also see with hindsight, that God uses this situation to separate the wheat from the weeds. God's promise was to Abram and his offspring. Not to his nephew... not to his servant...but to his own son. This situation causes a dividing line that separates the two. Both Abram and Lot are doing well in their lifestyle and inventory, but from now it will not be together.

Releases Lot to choose

With all of this angst and conflict, Abram chooses peace... Jesus honours peacemakers with the mark of family.

Bible Reference
Matthew 5:9

Abram chooses peace... to make peace... maintain peace... actively pursue peace. Peace first, and the principle that Jesus taught is that this choice offers us a place in the family of God. Abram chooses peace generously.

Abram allows Lot to be right, even when it takes two camps to fight. He does this by giving Lot first choice, his choice, any choice
>It is a generous act...
>It is a gracious act...
>It is the act of one who blesses...

Where can I see the invitation to be a peacemaker in my life?

How hard is it for me to allow others to be right, even when they are not?

It is the act of one who refuses to selfishly look after number one or demand to hold onto the position of power. It is the act of one who is not grabbing and taking and accumulating. It sounds like the Name of the

Lord and the nature of Jehovah whom Abram calls on. This is rubbing off on Abram.

How can I hang out with God more... and have his company infuse into my soul?

There is a shift. There is a reflection of the relationship on the inside, that is leaking out into his world, and his life, and changing the way he does relationships. Abram is willing to take a hit, if that is the way it works out. He releases Lot to choose. And predictably, Lot chooses what looks good, better, best. But it is only best on the surface.

He chooses the greener pasture... but it is not the healthiest choice, either socially or spiritually. Lot chooses to live among the cities of the plain... and he pitches his tents near Sodom. And there-in lies a problem. The people of Sodom were selfish... corrupt... immoral... grabbers. This is the place where Lot chose to put down his roots.

Dr Caroline Leaf is a clinical neuroscientist specializing in research in psychoneurobiology. She has a saying:
"We cannot change the people around us... but we can change the people around us..."

Lot was not willing to change the type of people he hung around with. What was in them... started to leach into him. He became a cultural chameleon. He didn't look any different to his environment. Abram, however, chose to be different. He hung around with God, and what was in God started to infuse into him. Abram is starting to stand out, different from the cultures and lifestyles around him. He is starting to carry himself with a divine distinctive.

Do I carry a Divine Distinctive, rather than being a cultural chameleon?

Rather than conforming, he chooses to do life differently. He couldn't necessarily change the people around him, and how they did life... that's their choice. But he could change the way *he* did life. He chose to do life with God.

Bible Reading
Genesis 13:14-18

Look around

Do you notice that the way God is talking with Abram, is building on what has been said before... expanding his understanding and the extent of his promise. Now God extends an invitation to Abram. "Look around... North; South; East and West... as far as you can see..." God tells Abram, "This is what I am gifting to you and your family... your offspring... forever."

Offspring that will be like the particles of dust on the earth. If we could count the specks of dust on the earth, we would have an idea of the extent of this promise who will occupy this inheritance. The very idea of trying to count the specks of dust on the earth is ludicrous! But it is the preposterous nature of the task, that is exactly the point.

Abram is a name that means exalted father. This is the assurance that Abram would be that father: an exalted father; a father of a nation that would be as extensive as the dust on the earth. That's a big promise!

Length & Breadth of the Land

Then God invites Abram, not just to look, but to walk through this promised land. To pound the pavement of the land that will be occupied by his family as a nation. He invites Abram to step it out. Walk the length and breadth of all that he had just looked at. Step out and walk through the tract of land that God is gifting his family with.

The plainlands along the Jordan were "well-watered", like the garden of Eden or like Nile delta of Egypt. This promise is of fertility and abundance. Do you remember how, generations later... the same invitation was given to the Israelites as they left Egypt and were preparing to occupy this promise that was given to Abram?

Joshua and Caleb and ten other tribal heads of Israel were invited into the same land, to walk through it, to walk through it and search it out... to explore it... to notice it... to discover it's richness.

Bible Reference
Numbers 13:1-23

The spies came back with produce, and bunches of grapes that could only be carried on a pole between two men. This same invitation is given to Abram right at the start. Go... walk... explore... notice. And I wonder if, by stepping out the promise, this embedded its reality into his heart. I wonder if, as he was walking, he was praying blessing and dedicating this land for what it would mean for future generations... generations from his household.

Imagine the wonder and reverence and astonishment in his heart as he realised that God is giving all this... to him... and his family. Such generosity. It reflects the generous nature of God.

Do I have a promise from God that I am still waiting for?
How could I look at it, or walk around it, in a way that will embed it confidently into my soul?

Everything that Abram deferred to Lot in an act of peace would be returned, restored, established, by the grace of God. God said that if he could see it, He was giving it to Abram. So... if Abram could see the cities and pastures of the plainlands, they were his... even those areas that Lot had claimed for himself. We cannot, with a sincere and genuine heart, out-give God. We cannot. It cannot be done.

Lived and occupied
Then we are told that Abram lived at Hebron. He pitched his tents. He put down his tent-pegs as a stake in the land of promise. He occupied it, as if it was his own. Something had already been transacted in the spiritual and now he is starting to walk in that promise... in faith. Yet it still had to be outworked in many ways. There is a lot left undone as yet... but Abram still believes.

The passage is wrapped up with Abram building an altar. Five times it is recorded that Abram builds an altar. He does this as a marker of significance, a new place, a new encounter, a new revelation. Recording and marking an important revelation, or lesson, or moment.

Over and over... a sacrifice is required. To record Abram's repentance, to remove the distance between him and his friendship with God and his desire to please God with his worship. In this ancient era, the patriarch of the household was both head of the clan, and they also acted in the office as priest.

God did not have a designated priesthood at this time. That came later when he appointed Aaron, (Moses' brother) and the Tribe of the Levites to serve in the Temple. Ancient times, ancient story. Each family's father took on that role of priest. Abram is serious about this priestly role. He took God seriously. He was genuine about it. This is something God desires of his friends. A genuine, generous authentic heart that respects and honours God and takes his relationship with God seriously.

Final thoughts...
Even though Abram is identified as a Friend of God, he didn't get it right all the time. Yet the encouragement we find in this story is that although Abram did get off track, God was still there, and he made choices to come back to the heart of God. Abram saw God's good intentions for his life. God was with Abram as their relationship was restored and rebuilt and enriched.

And this happened even when all those around him was choosing something quite different. Such as the choices made by Lot. He chose to blend in... to be a cultural chameleon

In 2021 an American study noted that 69% of Americans self-identify as Christians; however, of those only 6% of those who call themselves 'Christians' holds a biblical world view.[iii]
There are some disturbing stats around studies on Pornography.

Like 78% of American young people from 18-24 years in churches consume porn.

Australia is right in that mix. The 'Centre for Human Dignity' released a paper on "Pornography as a Public Health Issue" [iv] *and identified that Australia is the 8th largest consumer of pornography in the world.*

When there is no distinction in the way we think, rates of anxiety, depression, divorce, conflict, use of pornography, addictions... we have lost our Divine Distinctive. We have become Cultural Chameleons... we look like our surroundings. When I say "we", I identify with the church, the bride of Christ.

God wants our life to be better than that... healthier than that... more alive than that.

He wants us to trust him... that God is our shield
He wants to bless us... God wants to be our very great reward...
He desired that we carry this Divine Distinctive that is empowered to do life differently.

That is the blessing... blessing that does not just mean more stuff. It means doing life together... with God along the journey of our life.

Abram was learning to walk in this Divine Distinctive.
Abram chose peace: being a peacemaker was his distinctive.
Abram chose to worship only God: that was his distinctive.
Abram chose to not take on the colour and shape of the culture around him.
Abram chose to believe God, even when the promise was still a long way off.

And perhaps these are some of the qualities that makes Abram notable as a friend of God.

Prayer:

Father God, we thank you for the privilege to walk alongside you as a friend and our very great reward. Thank you that you give us your Holy Spirit to empower us to do life differently from those around us, and we don't have to blend in. Help us to be people who choose peace and make peace with those around us as much as it depends on us. Help us not to be cultural chameleons, looking like those around us, but that we would make choices that gives us a Kingdom cultural distinctive to honour your name.

In Jesus Name, Amen.

3.

Abram – The Just

Where we have been...
We see Abram was learning to walk in a Divine Distinctive, different from the cultures around him, and these are the qualities God is looking in a friend. Abram chose to be a peacemaker... that was his distinctive. Abram chose to worship only God... that was his distinctive. Abram chose to believe God, even when the promise is still a long way off.

In contrast, Lot – Abram's nephew, became a cultural chameleon and chose to take on the colour and shape of the culture around him. Lot pitches his tents near Sodom, and because Lot is Abram's family, this becomes part of the landscape that Abram is now interacting with. They went their separate ways, but they haven't disowned each other.

When the kids were younger, we were a camping family. There was a beautiful place with a creek where we would visit. We regularly saw platypus playing, beautiful birds – eagles and kingfishers and fairy-wrens. One day, it was hot, and the kids were swimming and playing in the creek. Some yelled out, "There's a snake!"
It was one of those moments when life slows in fast forward. Our eldest son got out of there, walking on water. Our other son levitated up the other side of the bank. And our youngest daughter was left standing in the middle of the creek, looking around dazed, "Whaaat?"
I saw our eldest son turned around. He looked at where his sister was, and he looked at where the snake was... and he went back in to draw her out of danger. Despite the risk... he went back in to retrieve his family.

Today we see a situation where Abram did the same. Despite the risk, he went in to retrieve his family. And the situation revolves around Lot, and the challenging circumstance of war.

War is traumatic, it is destructive, it is devastating. War is part of the human story. Conflict and fights happen at a household level, at a community level, and at regional and national levels. The account is Genesis 12 gives a summary of wars in this region during Abram's time there. This is about regional conflict. Remember, Ancient story... Ancient times. The Kings described here are not national sovereigns, but more like tribal chiefs. They are like the mayors of cities, rather than kings of nations or empires.

The account in Genesis 14 starts by naming and explaining the political alliances of the communities around the area. Four kings of four cities built a strong alliance, led by the king of Elan, Kedorlaomer (pronounced: Kay-door-lay-a-more). The Alliance of Four move in war against five other cities, which included the communities of Sodom and Gomorrah. They won this war, and for twelve years these five other cities have been subject to the strongest of these Alliance of Four.

Then king of Elan, Kedorlaomer headed the Alliance of Four to pursue a campaign to control the whole region. The king of Sodom, and the king of Gomorrah, along with their allies, marched out against the king of Elam and his allies — five subjugated kings try to stand against the strong Alliance of Four. And it doesn't go well, for a number of reasons.

Bible Reading
Genesis 14:10-20

Discerns which is his fight

Last week we saw Abram has risen to be a wealthy man with a lot of stuff. But he has not acquired the status of the regional kings. His community is small – 318 fighting age men. When compared to those around him Abram's little tribe is insignificant. It is fair to assume he might have had up to 600-1000 people who are his responsibility. Abram has his own alliances that are mentioned.

Ancient story... Ancient times. Yet some things are familiar. The oppression is familiar. The powerful alliances subjugate the weaker ones. The big are winning and becoming bigger, the others are suffering and losing. But I noticed Abram hasn't got involved in the politics of the region. He has stayed out of it. Until...

Until something happens that makes him discern that this is his fight. And that something is when it involves his family; then it does become his fight.

What injustices do I witness, that really presses a sore point in my heart? How could I add my hand to this fight for what is just?

I think it is worth noting that if Abram had already been exhausted – spending his mental, omotional, physical and financial resources fighting other people's battles, he would not have had the energy to pursue this particular fight, which is important to him. The injustice of slavery, the life and freedom of his nephew was at stake. That is what he is fighting for... he is fighting for justice.

Have I considered what is my actually fight, or do I take on everyone else's battles?

How would I discern which is my fight to fight for?

Doesn't hesitate

Then, in spite of the odds against him, Abram doesn't hesitate to go fight this fight. He gathers those born of his 'household', those who were part of his own mini tribe. 318 men and pursues those who have taken Lot and his family.

I had never particularly taken noticed that this is a victory in the league of the famous victory of the Judge Gideon.

Bible Reference
Judges 7

Gideon was in charge of 32000 men of Israel, and God whittles his army down to 300. Gideon's 300 men routed the Midianite army outnumbered 4:1, on the directive of God.

Abram does this first. He sets a precedence of fighting for right and partnering with God to be part of a miraculous outcome. Abram doesn't baulk at the odds. He doesn't send his men off to do the dirty work. He is not an armchair warrior, but is in there himself, in the fray. His 318 men stand against the Alliance-of-Four who have dominated the region (including the large, prosperous, influential cities of Sodom and Gomorrah), for over a decade. We don't know exactly what ratio they were up against, but we know without God, the odds of successfully securing this fight, was impossible.

Decisive victory

This was a decisive victory, yet we are barely given a foot note of what this battle looked like. It says Abram divided, routed, pursued, and recovered. He divided his men into pods – what he did, was considered and strategic, under the cover of night. He attacked the problem – they didn't hold back but went in with everything. He routed them – they overwhelmed the opposition, sent them running. He pursued them – he didn't leave them scattering like cockroaches but kept after them until the goal was achieved of bringing back all that was taken.

When there is a mention of actual places, I like to check what that looked like. My assumption was that they probably trailed them for 20 km or so. Which would be a good effort in my mind. Actually, Abram's base camp to north of Damascus is a distance of over 350 km. That's another level of fight. Persistent and dogged.

Abram recovered all the goods and brought back his relative Lot and his possessions, together with the women and the people of the conquered cities. Did you notice that Abram didn't just rescue Lot, but also, all the people of Sodom and Gomorrah. He saved cities of people that we might be tempted to think were not worth rescuing. He didn't judge or single some out as worthy and others as unworthy. He came back with all of them.

Abram and his people didn't give up... they didn't give out. They kept going until the job was done. Abram kept fighting until his family was safe.

Bible Reading
Genesis 14:17-20

King and Priest of Salem

Abram returns from this great victory as a hero. He had saved a whole city of people, the other families, not just his own loved one. It was not just people he retrieved, but the entire loot that had been taken from the cities that were raided, including the affluent places of Sodom and Gomorrah.

Then there is a surprising meeting of the kings in the valley of Shaveh. Perhaps this meeting is why this place was known as the Kings' Valley. The king of Sodom is there, saved by Abram and his little squad. But there is another king who is at this gathering: the King of Salem, whose name was King Melchizedek. Melchizedek is an old Canaanite name meaning "My King is [the god] Sedek" or "My King is the God Righteousness". Salem means peace and is the ancient name for Jerusalem.

Bible Reference
Psalm 77:2

So here we have a man who is identified as the King of the City of Peace. He is also a priest of Elyon – the Hebrew name for Supreme God Most High. Melchizedek goes to meet Abram in the Valley of Shaveh – which is a name that means the "plain that makes equality". When we put that all together, we have a king of peace, and a priest of the supreme God of righteousness, who meets Abram on a level plain of equality, while he shares bread and wine, and blessed him with a beautiful benediction:

"Blessed be Abram of the most high God, possessor of heaven and earth and blessed be the most high God, which hath delivered thine enemies into thy hand." (KJV)

None of this seems like a random co-incidence to me.

Symbol of Messiah

The king and priest Melchizedek is a striking prophetic encounter with the type and order of Messiah. Some people believe that Melchizedek was actually a manifestation of Jesus in ancient times. Such an appearance is called a "Christophany" – a physical appearance of Christ before his incarnation. Hmm... that's possible, but Melchizedek is referred to as a king and a priest... someone who occupied and lived in an ancient city with these very human roles. He didn't just miraculously appear for this one encounter. I'm more inclined to agree with the understanding that Melchizedek was a real person who was a type, or a symbol, a prophetic representation of Jesus as Messiah who was to come.

    a king of peace,
    a priest of the supreme God of righteousness,
    one who meets us all on a level plain of equality,
    one who shares bread and wine with us,
    and one who blesses us. Messiah.

Hebrews chapters 5, 6 & 7 offer a beautiful commentary on the symbolism of Melchizedek. I encourage you to read this...

Bible Reference
Hebrews 5, 6, 7

Jesus is our king of peace, and he is our priest of the Supreme God of Righteousness. As the writer of Hebrews declares: "You are a priest for ever after the order of Melchizedek."

Submits a tithe

Melchizedek reaches out to Abram at this meeting of the Kings. Abram responds by acknowledging the presence of God in this great, and miraculous victory, which saved the life and freedom of his nephew, and the life and freedom of these cities. They were saved from oppression.

We've already identified that Abram carried the role of priest in his family tribe as part of this ancient culture. He takes that role seriously. Here he submits to a higher-order priest and respectfully acknowledges God's favour in this endeavour. Abram receives the blessing from Priest Melchizedek, and then he responds by offering him a tenth of everything that had been acquired on this campaign.

Notice the order...
Abram is already blessed... he received the blessing from Melchizedek, and he responds with a grateful heart... a heart full of gratitude. He gives ten percent. This is the same principle that Moses instituted as the tithe, which is the amount that the people were to bring as an offering to God at the tabernacle.

We are seeing many things in Abram's life become the precedence for the Law of Moses. Abram is recognising the blessing of God in his life, by offering a tithe, ten percent of everything he had acquired, to the priest of the Most Supreme God of Righteousness.

The same principles apply to the offerings that we offer. The offering of a tithe is really to God, not the king or priest... but they become the custodians of these offerings. Ten percent. That principle still applies. The order is also the same: we are blessed, and we give out of a heart full of gratitude.

Do I offer a 10% tithe to God out of a heart of gratitude?

We don't tithe to be blessed. It is recognising what God has already done and is already doing, and we give out of a heart of gratitude regardless of whether we see the fulness of that yet. At this point so many things were still in the future for Abram, but he still gives out of his relationship... his friendship with God.

Bible Reading
Genesis 14:21-24

God first

So now Abram has more stuff. Cities of stuff! Retrieved as loot from this campaign. As a victor of a great battle, he was entitled to keep it all. This was all his, by rite of conquest. Yet we see Abram is careful in the way that he handles this victory... and the loot. As we have seen his first port of call is to offer ten percent as an offering to the priest of God. That is his priority... God is first.

When I experience victories... do I acknowledge God as my first port of call?

Distributed fairly

Then he distributes a share to his allies. They were given their cut. But then we see that he returns the rest of what was taken, both people and loot, to the king of Sodom. The king of Sodom offers Abram the option to keep all the loot and just return the people to their homes. He could have built his rather small tribe to a significant player in the local politics. He could have multiplied his own inventory to a new level of stuff. But as tempting as that might have been, Abram says no.

Faith in God's faithfulness

Abram resolved not to take a short cut. He was not going to give the King of Sodom the opportunity to take the credit for what was God's victory and God's blessing.

Do I have absolute confidence in the faithfulness of God in my life?

Sodom's reputation goes before him. Corruption might build inventory, but it does not build blessing. Only God does that. Abram does not want to compromise God's blessing in his life by being a grabber.

God has already told him that he was be a conduit of blessing to all the people of the earth through him. Abram holds an unwavering belief in God's faithfulness to his promises. Abram doesn't need the goods of corrupt kings... or he might become corrupt like them.

Abrams knows he needs to protect his relationship with God to experience his blessing. He holds to his integrity, and his faith, and his solid conviction of God's faithfulness

Abram has stepped out the promise God gave him. He has walked the length and breadth of the land. He knows what the promise looks like, and he doesn't need the loot of corrupt kings to make it happen. He will give his all and trust God will make up the difference. That to me... because he got that straight, this perhaps is the greatest victory of this conquest.

Final thoughts...

As we walk along-side Abram, we are witnessing more of the qualities that God has articulated that he wants in his friends. Abram is one who fought for justice – he put himself out there correcting injustice. He went to retrieve one family member from danger, which sounds remarkably like a shepherd who goes looking to retrieve the one lost and displaced sheep. He ended up saving a number of cities... even cities like Sodom and Gomorrah which we probably don't think are worth saving. Yet this sounds remarkably like the God who took mercy on the city of Nineveh, and made sure Jonah went to intercede for it.

Abram gave generously out of what he had, with the conviction that God would make up the difference. It would not be the wealth of corrupt Kings that would make him rich but the gracious hand of his faithful God.

I was thinking about this idea that we give everything... and God makes up the difference. At one church we were part of, we held a charity auction. One of the people in the congregation was an accomplished artist and had donated a wonderful canvas – a little abstract, but a powerful image, loaded with meaning around the suffering of Christ. This canvas was to be auctioned.

Our youngest daughter was in Grade 2, and she had heard a family friend say that he had really admired this painting, so she determined that she would buy it for him. She cleaned out her piggybank and she came with her life savings to buy this painting. This was everything she had.

But her twenty dollars wasn't enough. The price went up: $70 – $100 – $150... The price was still going up. But what I noticed was that where she had given everything.... and it wasn't quite enough; her dad took over... and he made it enough.

I think that canvas went for something like $370 ... not exactly high-end art. But it probably wouldn't have mattered who came to that auction that day, bidding for that painting. This little girl had resolved, to generously give this to a friend. She put her all in, and it was her dad who saw her heart, and made sure she got to give him his painting. For many years, that painting hung in his office. He may still have it.

Sometimes we give everything... and we truly believe that will do it, and yet we find in reality, it falls short by a long way, and it is not enough. But God, as our father, steps in, takes our offering and builds on it... and makes it enough.

Whether it is a resolve to fight for what is just... even when it is a fight that is ridiculously against the odds. Whether it is a resolve to generously give our best to God first. Whether it is a resolve to not take a shortcut, to help God along... but to allow his hand to be generously demonstrated in our life.

God wants us to be that sort of friend... a friend to puts everything in. He wants us to fight against those things that are not just. He wants us to acknowledge him in the remarkable victories when he makes up the difference. He wants to bless us, by doing life together... with God along the journey of our life.

Abram chose to fight for justice. Abram acknowledges and seriously honours God in his life. He would not take anything that would draw the glory away from the hand of God. Abram chose to acknowledge God... by tithing to Melchizedek, the king and priest of Salem. Abram chose not to take a shortcut by believing in the gain of corrupt kings, but instead he chose to believe in the faithfulness of God. Perhaps these are some of the qualities that makes Abram a friend of God.

Prayer:

Father God, thank you that you desire us to walk in fellowship with you, side-by-side throughout our life journey. Help us to attend to those things that you have laid on our heart, where you want us to fight for justice. Help us to discern where you desire us to pursue the enemy and where you want us to wait. Give us courage to pursue a world that is just and not ruled by corruption and oppression.

In Jesus Name, Amen.

4.
Abraham – The Obedient

Where we have been...
We see Abram definitely carried a Divine Distinctive that is different from the cultures around him.
Abram chose to be a peacemaker... that was his distinctive.
Abram chose to pursue justice rather than more stuff... that was his distinctive.

Yet as we look into the life of Abraham, we find that even though he is a man who is famously known as a friend of God, we've discovered that he didn't always get things right. He made mistakes. He was learning that God was El Shaddai – the Most High God. Sometimes he didn't always hit the mark. But there were some essential qualities in Abram that God found was the heart of a true friend.

We've seen stories of Abram interacting with Pharaohs, and Kings, and tribal chiefs, at a tribal and community level. Going off to war. Today's story zooms into his family to find what is happening at home inside his tents.

Bible Reading
Genesis 16:1-5

Delay takes its toll
Ancient story... Ancient times. The idea of waiting is uncomfortable, yet it is probably familiar to us.

Even in the small things... like at the checkout when it takes a long time to process the small shop of the lady in front. I've noticed times when I was uncomfortable waiting, until they swapped out the service-attendant for someone with more experience and things began to move more quickly.

That's a small thing. Big things... life things, are even more so.

Delay is a challenge that can cause us to waver. Abram has a promise that he will become a father of a great nation. He believed it. But month after month after month, his wife Sarai is not pregnant. For ten years of months... she is not pregnant.

> How disappointing...
> How disheartening...
> How devastating...

It takes its toll, on Sarai more than Abraham it seems.

Described it as failure

Every month... another period comes... not pregnant again. One hundred and twenty months! That's a lot of delay. Sarai interprets all this delay as her failure. She has failed to deliver. Her disappointment and pain taints the way she sees herself, and then it taints the way she sees God. The Lord has failed to deliver. She blames God, who has kept this blessing from her. It is a suggestion as old as the Garden of Eden. God is holding out on me. It is his fault.

Deviated from the plan with a work-around

Sarai took a leaf out of the book of the cultures around her. Ancient story... Ancient times. Polygamy and surrogacy were common practices. Slaves were property to do whatever you required. This was a socially acceptable work-around, to have a slave bear children for you. But I notice that Abram wasn't just the sperm-donor in this situation. He took Hagar to be his 'wife'. He married her. Work-arounds might seem like it is using initiative. In practical matters, sometimes they are necessary. This is creative use of available resources. We all have examples of working through ways of how we are going to do things with limited resources and engineering creative solutions. But unfortunately, a work-around when it comes to the specific plans of God will always create problems.

Am I frustrated by delays of promises I have from God?

How can I wait without trying to implement a work-around?

When delays cause us to try and jam open a door that is already a promise from God, it is an act of disobedience. If God says trust and wait, and we don't... that is not initiative... that is faithlessness, lacking faith. Lacking confidence that God is good for his word. God is trustworthy... he wants us to be confident in our relationship with him. He wants us to rest in his promises, not try and engineer them.

I had a promise from God that he was moving me into a pastoring appointment. But it was not coming to be. In fact, everything seemed to be moving backwards. I acknowledged that time was not on my side: I'm doing this as a mature person. One night I was walking outside, letting off steam, so frustrated! Then I stopped and I checked myself.
The Holy Spirit had spoken to me and said, "Not if, but when...." I reminded myself that these were His words, not mine. I reminded myself that God is good for His word: He had said this, so he is faithful to what he says. I reminded myself, from this story, that even if I am a

hundred like Sarah, the timing of God is perfect." I paused again and placed myself back in a place of trust. "God knows what this will look like. He is never late..."

Strangely enough... within a fortnight of that internal conversation, I was contacted by a little country church and things began to shift. Within a few months, I was appointed as their pastor. The timing of God is never late. Sarah helped remind me in that in moments of frustration, it is best not to try and jam open doors to make things happen.

Despised in her heart

This situation with Hagar gets ugly. Hagar is now Abram's wife: the pregnant wife. The dynamics change in the household, particularly in her relationship with Sarai. Where once Hagar was a trusted handmaiden, now she becomes entitled. Now she scorns Sarai who has been her mistress. Now she despises Sarai in her heart

"I have succeeded where you have failed"

"I am better than you"

"I deserve more than just being a handmaiden"

"I am entitled... You should serve me"

The intention of building a family through surrogacy goes out the tent-flap. Even equality is not enough for Hagar. Hagar will not share her pregnancy. Perhaps she will not share her husband. Life in the household of Abram is now very unstable and conflicted. Sarai not only blames God, but she also blames Abram for what has happened as well. She forgets this work-around was her idea

Bible Reading
Genesis 16:6-16

God who sees me

The name that Hagar calls God is 'El Roe'. It is a beautiful name that I often go back to: The God who sees me. It can mean I can call on the name of God who sees me in trouble... in conflict. It can mean I can call on the name of God who sees me alone and abandoned. It can mean I can call on the name of God who sees me when life is full and abundant... in all of life's circumstances.

Right at the beginning, Abram discovered God is not like the gods and idols of his father. This God is a god who speaks; a god who hears. And He is also the God who sees... even when we forget that He sees.

What is it like to know God sees me?

God saw Hagar, but he also saw Sarai in all of her heartache and disappointment. God saw Sarai as she tries to solve an unsolvable problem. God saw Sarai as she abuses Hagar, and is a bully, and is cruel to her. The forgetting was not God's. God had not forgotten Sarai.

When have I forgotten God sees me?

The plan had not changed. It was still in place. God is always true to his word. The forgetting was in Sarai's court. She had forgotten that she was accountable for her choices. She blamed God. She blamed Abram. She blamed Hagar. She had forgotten that God still sees her. This was a woman who had been seen by men all her life because she was incredibly beautiful, but now she forgets that it is more important to know, first and foremost that God sees us. Just because we forget... it doesn't mean God stops seeing us.

When we flee

Hagar flees her home. What had been designated as a place of safety and protection had become intolerable. She is pregnant. She is vulnerable. She goes along the road through Shur. This is south, on the way to Egypt. Her intent is to go back to Egypt, back to her home country and culture.

When have I tried to run away?

After she had walked over 100 km's. She rests at an oasis in the wilderness, the springs of Shur. In this place... a place of running, of escape, in flight... an angel of the Lord hears her misery and sees her plight. He comes and speaks to her. God asks a question... "Hagar, slave of Sarai, where have you come from, and where are you going?" God's questions are not to gather information that he doesn't know. Of course, God knows where is from and where she is going. His questions help clarify for the person what is really going on.

Hmm. "Hagar, slave of Sarai." God hasn't called her Abram's wife, but her designation is still slave. In fact, Abram isn't mentioned at all. She was Sarai's handmaiden, and that has not changed. This suggests to me that this is between Sarai and Hagar. God sees her in the reality of her situation.

Then the angel says, Go back to your mistress and submit to her.

Hmm. This is a problem for me. In my counselling work, I would never recommend that someone intentionally go back to an abusive situation if they are trying to extricate themselves from that situation. I would facilitate their independence and offer resources to find a place of safety.

Here I need to pause: Ancient times; Ancient story. Just because it is recorded in the Bible in this ancient account, that Hagar is to return to an abusive situation, this doesn't make it a rule for life across all spectrums of humanity across all time. It is a snapshot of this person's story.

This account does not mean God condones bullying behaviour or is endorsing abuse. Never! God's nature is kind, loving, protective. However, it appears that in this ancient time, this was the best course for Hagar and the baby that she carried. She was vulnerable, she was pregnant, she was alone, she was out in the middle of nowhere. God's kindness saw her, when no one else saw her. God's love was protecting Hagar, even when Abram had dropped the ball, and Sarai was throwing them at her. Nothing about this picture of Abram or Sarai in this situation is glamorous or appropriate, and yet El Roe... "The God who Sees" ... sees Hagar. He sends an angel to her side and firmly tells her what she must do: Stop running.

When we follow with faith
God had made a promise to Abram that he would bless his family; this now includes the child that Hagar carries. The angel gives Hagar a picture of this blessing. This child would be the carrier of God's blessing too.

He will carry a name that God had given him: Ishmael, God hears. We have a God who sees, and a God who hears. God sees and hears us, even in the ugly times of our life... even in our misery. Even in the times when we have become wedged in situations that have been born out of circumstances, from choices that are not our best selves. God sees and hears.

Hagar is now the carrier of a promise... for herself and her son. This was not the plan God was speaking out when he gave Abram his promise. But God works with our failure, and our detours, and our deviations and brings us back to himself. Ishmael would become a great nation.

Did you know that Ishmael had 12 sons, who became 12 rulers of 12 tribes. God's promise of greatness to Hagar and her son was genuine. It was a promise God later confirmed to Abram. Ishmael would become great, but not as a nation of peace, but of conflict and war. Not a nation of reconciliation, but a 'wild donkey', a picture of unruliness, untameable strength, and hostility.

So, Hagar returns home... to Sarah. Not in arrogance, not thinking highly of herself but thinking more highly of God. In faith, she follows the message God gave her through his angel. Was it easy? I would say not. Yet she follows in faith, believing that God sees even her. Her lowliness would not be forever. God has another, alternative reality that he sees for her, and it will come to pass.

How can I turn around and follow with faith?

Bible Reading
Genesis 17:1-24

God initiates covenant

There is a progression in the relationship between God and Abram. There is now an agreement that takes this friendship to a new level of intimacy. The promise has progressed.

The idea of covenant did not start with Abram. Covenant was a standard way of binding contracts between families, between neighbours, between tribes: "I will agree to this... and you will agree to this. If you don't keep these terms... you will die; and if I don't keep these terms... I will die."

They didn't mess around. If you put your word and your "handshake" on something in covenant... it was binding. Binding on your life. Abram was fully aware of the protocols of entering into covenant. He would have done this many times with his allies and kings, neighbours and business associates.

Abraham's commitment

But a covenant with God? God coming down to his level... reaching out to Abram? Yes! This is putting blood to the talk. God is putting a seal of covenant to the promise.

God has a history of coming into covenant with people. He did this with Adam. Adam broke the terms, and death was the outcome. That wasn't unfair, they are the terms of an agreed covenant. Mortality became a human reality.

Bible Reference
Genesis 2:8-9;15-17

God also made a covenant with Noah.

Bible Reference
Genesis 9:1-15

Now God invites Abram to be part of a covenant relationship as well. The first part of this covenant is that God changes Abram's name. Not Abram – "exalted father", but Abraham – "father of many nations". God's covenant was not with the old Abram, but with Abraham, a man who is changed. A man who is His friend. A friend who is faithful in his heart.

Sarai's name is also changed, from a generic term of endearment 'Sarai' to 'Sarah' – "Princess". Loved, cherished, a mother of princes and kings.

Abraham falls face down. He agrees to enter this covenant. He commits his life, his family, his household, his small tribe to this covenant.

Sealed with circumcision

Ancient times; ancient story. Remember the culture around Abraham's is rife with idol worship. Idol worship required a demonstration of devotion to their deities. One way they would do that was by cutting. The greater the devotion, the greater the cutting. But there were no parameters to say how much cutting is enough. Do you keep going, even to the point of mutilation? If this is an accepted form of worship in this culture, how does one demonstrate devotion sufficiently? It becomes a point of uncertainty that you might never do enough or be acceptable to the idol you worship.

Abraham's relationship with God is different to that. God puts a boundary around this. The sign of Abraham's devotion is just one cut... personal and unseen. That is enough. There is the sheading of blood. This is the seal to this agreement. This is the signature on this covenant, that they are both entering into.

The account says: "On that very day...". The covenant was agreed to – and Abraham is immediately obedient to the terms of this covenant. Abraham circumcised himself and every male in his household. We know that is at least 318 men, plus boys from eight days old. That's a lot of foreskins. Abraham is in. Obedient to the agreed terms. 100%.

Much of the story of Abraham speaks to our own relationship with God. There is a new covenant God invites us to enter into with him through Jesus. Paul's letter to the churches in Galatia offers a beautiful parallel to this part of Abraham's story to our Christian experience.

Bible Reading
Galatians 4:22-31

Children of Promise
Abraham understands there will be a son, a freeborn son who is still yet to come. A son who will be born of a promise. A son who is born supernaturally, not a decision made from him as a biological father. A son who is born after this covenant was enacted. A son who is born – not of a slave, but freeborn. A son of promise. A son of covenant.

Paul describes how we carry that same promise in our relationship with Jesus. That we are carriers of freedom, not bound by slavery, corruption, or protocols of society and culture. We are free and empowered to make better choices; healthier choices; life honouring choices, God honouring choices.

Do I really live as a free born?

What parts of my life are still under the bond of slavery?

The new covenant that we now are invited to be part of is not sealed by our devotion, by cutting and cutting and cutting. Now, not even one small cut demanded by a law, but sealed by the cutting of our heart in repentance.

The remarkable thing about the covenant that God made with Abraham is that God took upon Himself the punishment or the consequences if this covenant was broken.

A usual covenant agreed to the terms: 'If I don't keep this covenant... I die. If you don't keep this covenant... you die.' Standard contractual terms in this ancient culture. Yet God does something quite extraordinary in his covenant: God agreed to something profoundly gracious: 'If I don't keep this covenant... I die. If you don't keep this covenant... I die.'

God knew the covenant with his people would be broken and rather than throw up his hands in hopelessness, God took it upon Himself to pay the price of that contractual agreement, with his own life. Himself. He would pay this price.

What happens in me as I consider that God takes this covenant so seriously that He would take the consequences of breaking its terms upon Himself?

This is the blessing that would be passed to all humanity through Abraham's linage. That is the privilege of being children of promise, alive and born as free-born children of inheritance. This ancient story becomes a representation of our life with God... children of promise. Born into the family of God... free sons and daughters with an eternal inheritance

Conclusion: Abraham's friendship with God is sealed in a covenant. The old Abram gave way to frustrations and delays that were haunting Sarai. A son was born... out of slavery, out of frustration. The new Abraham believes the promise of an inheritance given to a free-born son and God and Abraham seal this covenant with a mark of their vow of commitment to each other in this agreement.

Final thoughts...

Part of my journey as a pastor is that when God started to talk to be about this, is that I really didn't want to. I was not interested.
When this idea first came up, I said to God, "You know I will if you want me to... it is just that I really don't want to. But feel free to change my 'want to'."
Sometimes just willing to be willing... is a place to begin. By the time it seemed like the promise would not come to pass, I really wanted to.
Yet for me, the anticipation of a promise and walking it out were two different places. When I started in my appointment as a pastor it was hard. Turning up was hard. Opening the doors was hard. Preaching on a Sunday to four people, one of which was my husband... that was hard. One of the significant things that made a shift for me, was changing my language from: "I should" to "I could." "I have to" to "I get to."
Over and over, I intentionally changed my language to "I get to!" I get to do this. I get to do this! God again needed to change my 'want to'! I understand that there were many factors that were part of what was

happening there. It took prayer, and wrestling, but I got to the point again where I really wanted to! I look back on that season in that Church, as beautiful, and rich, and rewarding.

I am so grateful I God enabled me to do that! I got to do that!

God wants us to be the sort of friend that puts everything in by obeying. Jesus said obedience is a mark of friendship.

Bible Reference
John 15:12-14

Obeying... not as slaves; not because we have to, or we should. Yes, sometimes obedience is pushing through and making better choices. Sometimes it is hard, and grind, and difficult. God is always moving us to a place of greater freedom. We are children of promise. He offers us this so we can engage in the life he has for us. Not because we have to, or we should, but because we have a good friend who loves us: we can, and we get to.

God chose to go into a covenant with Abraham... a covenant of love, friendship. Abraham chose to go into a covenant with God... a covenant of love, friendship. Abraham acknowledges and honours this covenant with God by obedience. This is another of those qualities that makes Abraham a friend of God.

Prayer:
Father God, we are grateful that you don't demand servitude, that you don't treat us like slave, but that you have entered into a covenant with us and call us friends and family. Help us to be faithful to you, even during those times when we don't want to. Please continue to move to a place of greater freedom. Help us to be willing to be willing, and that you will continue to draw us into a place of fresh love and revelation!
In Jesus Name, Amen.

5.

Abraham - The Merciful

Where we have been...

Abraham and Sarah found the waiting hard, and rather than waiting on the timing of God, Sarah tries to push open the door. Now we consider a story where Abraham was moved to pray into a situation which may seem contradictory to the loving attribute of God. It starts with fellowship and friendship. God is talking with Abraham.

This remarkable event begins as an ordinary day... a routine hot day when Abraham was just getting on with life... which was part of the waiting, when suddenly 'routine' is thrown out the window.

Bible Reading
Genesis 18:1-15

He saw three men

This account begins on an ordinary day. It's hot. It's routine. Abraham is just sitting in the entrance of his tent... trying to catch a breeze, when three visitors come to the tents of Abraham.

We are given the head's up that this was an appearance of "The Lord" – Jehovah. This is one of those appearances of the Lord that is hard to understand. Abraham has encountered God who speaks and sees. God has helped him in difficult situations. But this time 'The Lord' (singular) appeared to Abraham as three travellers. So why three persons? Was one of the visitors God and the other two angels? Or were there three angels as the Hebrew traditions suggests, and God was just present as the Invisible Spirit? It is also possible that what we have here is what is understood as a "theophany". That is a physical appearance of God: "theophany."

There is a very old Christian interpretation of this account – one that Augustine supported, that this was a manifestation of Trinity. Three persons but one Lord. However, there are many other interpretations, including traditional commentaries of Judaism who do not recognise a Triune God, nor that Jesus as Messiah would be part of this Trinity.

The idea of God walking, talking together, fellowshipping with each other, and including humans in the circle of their unity and fellowship is strange. Breaking bread together... eating and drinking and talking together. This idea, that God would choose to break bread with us, can be challenging.

What is it like to think of God as three visitors who will sit and talk and have dinner with me?

Tended to humble service

Yet Abraham is not shocked by this appearance of The Lord. He jumps up immediately and runs to meet them, eagerly offering them hospitality. He, himself, washes the feet of his visitors, in humble service. He kills a choice and tender calf (not a lamb or goat... but a calf... a higher level of generous hospitality). He calls on Sarah to cook some fresh bread... using three seahs of flour! That is about 23 litres, over and above what would be practically needed for 3 visitors... this was a feast! It is a liberal gesture; nothing is held back.

As I was reading this account it sounded to me like Jesus may have borrowed imagery Father Abraham and incorporated them into the story of the Good Father... and the prodigal son.
> The father running to meet his visitors...
> The father killing the fatted calf...
> The father serving a feast...

The father of nations reflecting the heart of God the Father... and in turn becomes a picture of the Good Father for us.

Took time to commune
And then the three visitors sit down together with Abraham and take time to visit and talk with him. It isn't rushed. They share and fellowship. Converse as friends.

How can I take more time to sit and talk with God?

As they talk together, another subject comes up, and this is a subject that is a little more sensitive.

Bible Reading
Genesis 18:9-15

Hope deferred
There has been a deferred hope that has been part of their life for the twenty-five years since Abram was called to leave his home country in Ur of the Chaldeans.

There is a proverb that talks about deferred hope:
Bible Reference
Proverbs 13:12

The Lord tells Abraham that the waiting is over. The first time Abraham was told this, he also had a less than glorious reaction.

Bible Reference
Genesis 17:17
Abraham had laughed at this idea. Sarah overhears the conversation with these three visitors, and she has the same response.

Bible Reference
Genesis 18:12
There seems to be an understanding that Abraham was laughing with joy, faith and pleasure while Sarah laughed in a mocking way.

Long past hope
The problem with this idea is that that the word used for both these laughing responses is identical:

tsâchaq (Strong Reference number: H6711)
It is described as to laugh outright in scorn; laugh, mock, play, make sport.

Same word – not one that is happy and full of faith, and one that is cynical and bitter. This idea was ludicrous for both of them. It wasn't a case of Abraham was holy, and Sarah scorned the idea. Humanly speaking, this was impossible. Ridiculous. Menopause had passed. Childbearing was off the table now.

Yet God says, despite circumstances He is a God who is good for his word. His word is not subject to the naturally possible. Both Abraham and Sarah knew this; for both of them, this was a difficult thing to get their head around.

Is anything too hard for the Lord? In fact, perhaps it was because it was humanly impossible, that the timing of this event was so important. This was a supernatural act.

It wasn't just a child God was birthing; it was the seed of a nation that would bless the whole of humanity down through the ages. This conception was divinely engineered because God was intervening in unusual ways. This was a spiritual agenda that this couple was invited to be part of.

God uses this specific phrase "Is anything too hard for the Lord?" twice in scripture. Once here... as the conception of the people of Israel. And then to the prophet Jeremiah when he is prophesying the invasion from Nebuchadnezzar and the restoration of Israel from exile.

Bible Reference
Jeremiah 32:27

"Is anything too hard for the Lord?" Both times, the plan looks impossible from the outside, but God is not bound by human limitations. God intends to use Abraham to bless all the people of the earth through him. It is a plan that prevails, even though it is impossible to those looking on.

Then straight out of this conversation of blessing and impossible impartation and restoration, another more sober conversation comes next. I wonder at the timing of these two events: one conversation is about new life, new birth, new beginnings; and another conversation is of death and destruction. It seems to me that they have to be connected. God first talks about enacting his enduring solution, before he addresses the alternate way of dealing with sin.

Bible Reading
Genesis 18:16-33

Deep seated Corruption

I confess I find the judgment visited on Sodom and Gomorrah difficult to understand. But it is important to remember: Ancient times; ancient story. I think a place to start is to clarify what the sin, or the brokenness of Sodom and Gomorrah was. There is an account of a ruthless sexual assault as the angels on assignment go into the city. This brutal behaviour is horrifying. Yet God identifies it is a symptom of the underlying pathology of their heart. God gave Ezekiel a summary of what really was the problem when he later compares Israel to the corruption that he witnesses in Sodom.

Bible Reading
Ezekiel 16:49-50

The people of Sodom were arrogant; haughty; overfed; unconcerned. They had no compassion and gave no assistance to the poor and needy.

How can I address those things in my life that were the sins of Sodom?

Do you notice that sexual sin is not mentioned here as God establishes what he found so repugnant? That might be what we focus on, yet for God, that didn't even rate a mention when he is diagnosing this problem to Ezekiel. There were a whole lot of detestable things going on, that were symptoms of this underlying pathology... this cancer of selfishness and arrogance.

These people lived a hedonistic lifestyle – full of overindulged appetites in every aspect of their lives... and yes, even their sexuality. They live their lives inwardly... not outwardly, with eyes that failed to see other people's needs. Or if they did see the poor and needy, they refused to move to help. They were selfish and arrogant. If you think Sodom was wiped out because of homosexuality you are mistaken. It had to do with their over-indulged hearts that were hard, and selfish, and couldn't care less about others. What God spoke to Ezekiel tells us that everything we see here in this community is the exact opposite of what God desires.

Bible Reference
Micah 6:8

To act justly... they corrupted justice and lived over-fed, selfish lives. To love mercy... they had no mercy but were unconcerned about the plights of the poor and needy... this is important in God's eyes. To walk humbly... they were arrogant and haughty. There was a basic standard of human dignity that they failed to reach or uphold. They fell short... completely... in every aspect of their lives.

Opportunity for change
Do you remember in the chapter about Abram – The Just, we have been told that the people of Sodom and Gomorrah were given an opportunity for change. God didn't just come in and wipe them off the map in a supernatural fire-storm. These are the cities that God had miraculously rescued from the hand of the oppressive Alliance of Four. God had intervened to save them. They had been given back their freedom, but they used that freedom to greedily self-indulge. They had been restored, but they used this restoration to rebuild to their own selfish agendas. They had experienced grace, but they used that grace for decadence.

Abraham's rescue had given them a second chance after 12 years of oppression. They knew about the God who had saved their families and all of their things... everything had been restored – nothing was missing. But they used their new-found freedom to turn in on themselves and ignore those who needed help.

When we think of the sins of Sodom and Gomorrah in these terms, it is a sobering reminder that God is a God of justice. It also comes as a caution, so that we don't become blind to our own short comings.

God listens to compassion

As these three visitors sit together, God talks to Abraham and shares his concerns about the heartless corruption that is witnessed in Sodom and Gomorrah. God's justice is fearsome, and yet he pauses to share what he is about to do, with Abraham. He is going to destroy these cities, because their corruption can no longer be maintained.

But Abraham doesn't just agree, he is moved to intercede for these cities. Not because he was whitewashing the corruption that was witnessed there, but because it is not just to have good swept away with the twisted and foul. Over and over Abraham intercedes...
>   Fifty...
>   Forty...
>   Thirty...
>   Twenty...
>   Ten...

Here we witness that Abraham's heart loves mercy. He intercedes so that for the sake of good, the cities would be saved.

If God was looking for good in our community... would he be able to count me?

God listens and changes his intent because of this conversation with Abraham. I also notice that Abraham wasn't involved in this fight on this occasion. It was not his role to rescue Lot this time. He has discerned that his participation was through prayer and intercession. It was his prayer that made a difference... and saved Lot.

One day I was hanging out the clothes, and my spirit became very agitated. I was unsettled and compelled to pray for my daughter who was away on a school excursion. The feeling of impending doom didn't go away. I tried to talk myself down... but it would not settle. I rang a friend, and we prayed together... and after we had prayed, that urgency settled.

I later shared with some ladies in a prayer group about this. This was unusual for me, and I was uncertain how to understand this. There is no grand story of a near miss, or a crisis averted. One lady just looked at me and shrugged, very matter of fact. "God showed you. You prayed. He addressed whatever was going on. Your daughter came home. Done."

Her mater-of-fact approach made it sound so normal. It wasn't an episode of generalised anxiety. God was sharing a matter that needed to be addressed, and he chose me to be part of what he was doing. I believe prayer makes a difference. That is part of the life we have been invited into as friends of God. He shares things with us. Sometimes we hear the story. Sometimes we don't. I've heard remarkable stories, where people were moved to pray with amazing results. But whether we know the back story or not, God is still inviting us to be part of what he is doing.

Bible Reading
Genesis 19: 23-29

Destruction

If the definition of sin is 'missing the mark', then this is a very powerful example of what unrestrained sin looks like. Failure to love; to reach out to help and care for others. Personal wants and desires only have priority. Abuses on a grand scale... and God was not okay with it.

If there had been just ten people who had honour in these cities, God would have saved the whole valley, yet God was unable to find even a remanent of integrity in these communities. Josephus records that the desolate ashen remains of the five aligned cities of the valley could be visited in his time. The region where Lot had moved to because it had been like the Garden of Eden, became barren, unproductive and desolate. Destruction had been complete.

Fire and brimstone

Brimstone is the old term for sulphur: "The stone that burns". Burning sulphur gives off the smell of rotten-egg gas. A hailstorm of sulphur is fiery, putrid and completely destructive. This has become the portrait of hell for us. A reminder of the consequences of choices that turn inwards. The consequences of living with choices that go against God and His intention for life. This physical event became a sober warning to the Israelites as God goes into to covenant with them through Moses.

Bible Reference
Deuteronomy 19:23-25

The Israelites understood that abandoning or breaking covenant has consequences of barrenness and destruction.

King David also used this imagery in Psalm 11

Bible Reference
Psalm 11:6-7

Each time fire and brimstone are mentioned in scripture, it is understood that it is coupled with God's heart of justice. Not as something that it is harsh and unfair; it is harsh and yet *completely* fair, coming from a divine heart that acts justly; loves mercy; walks humbly before God.

God never expects from us what he is not able to empower us with his Spirit. God is perfectly just, perfectly merciful, perfectly humble.

If we were able to stand on the mountain where Abram and Lot stood over-looking the valley that was once fertile like the Garden of Eden, or the Nile delta, towards those cities, we would now only see the rolling sands of desert and wilderness. Everything that was spoken has come to pass: Barrenness and destruction! That is a high price for selfishness and indulgence.

Escape felt like death
Only Lot and his family is offered the opportunity to be saved. Yet, even as Lot is being pulled from destruction, Lot begged to stay close to those lifestyle choices rather than make a clean break. Escape and leaving it all behind felt like it would kill him. He couldn't understand how leaving was a choice for life... and staying was a choice for death.

Where do I need to leave a situation that is against God's truth?

Longing for the deception

While Lot was living in the place of deception, the mercy of God is scorned. Lot's sons-in-law thought the angels were kidding. Their selfish hearts couldn't hear a warning, much less heed it. They chose to stay in a place that would destroy them.

Lot's wife, even though she was physically leaving the city, wasn't able to leave that way of life in her heart. Just like the Israelites wanted to go back to slavery in Egypt, Lot's wife wanted to go back to the slavery of that lifestyle…. and she turned to salt.

The deception of these places had such a grip… The lie was that staying in Sodom was really living; and leaving that behind was death. Yet the truth was… staying there was death, and escaping was an opportunity for a new life.

What parts of the old deception still have its hold over me?
How can I get help to leave that behind?

The last we hear of Lot he is living in a cave, isolated. Some traditions say Lot lived in poverty for the rest of his life, pining for the old things from that period when he lived in Sodom.

Are there things that I am pursuing and investing in, that will not last?

Lot has two sons: Moab and Ben-Ammi. From them came the tribes of the Moabites and Ammonites. These are names that come up often in the story of Israelites, as the enemies of the people of Israel. Lot's family did not take on the worship of the one true God of Abraham – who had been like a father to Lot, but rather this family continued to worship the detestable gods of Sodom and Gomorrah – particularly the gods of Chemosh and Molech. In the end, everything that Lot coveted and desired, was lost. Those things he invested in, did not... and could not last.

Final thoughts...

God visits Abraham and has significant conversations with him as his friend. The first is the announcement of the imminent birth of their son... a son of covenant, who would bring a line of blessing to all humanity. The second conversation is the disclosure of the outcry against the selfishness of Sodom.

Abraham intercedes for the good in those communities, yet there was not enough good to tip the scales of justice. I believe God is showing Abraham that the brokenness of humanity needs to be dealt with. It cannot, within any form of justice, be left unrestrained. It will either be dealt with by fire: cleansing and purifying. Or it will be dealt with by the coming of a child of promise... an alternate approach where the pain of that brokenness is taken away, and life of blessing is offered instead.

My father was talking with someone he knew, and in the course of the conversation this person said to him, "I have a lot of things that I expect to happen in my life because they keep me comfortable. I don't like to be uncomfortable, so I expect them to happen." Dad came away from that conversation with a deep sense that this was profound definition of 'selfishness'. The expectation of personal comfort supersedes all other experiences.

God wants us to be the sort of friend that looks out for other people, loves each other. Love each other even when it interferes with our personal comfort; even when it cuts across our own personal agendas and preferences. By loving each other, we love God in a profound way. This is another of those qualities that makes Abraham a friend of God.

Prayer:
Father God, we thank you that you are a merciful God, and you love justice and righteousness. As we reflect on this sobering story, Jesus we ask that you move our hearts to love each other with greater sincerity. Help us to address needs as we meet them in ways that are humble, and thoughtful, and kind, and compassionate. May we be one of those people that you can count to be a righteous person in our community... that we may be light in a dark place... and be a transformational catalyst where you have positioned us.
In Jesus Name, Amen.

6.

Abraham – The Faithful

Where we have been...
Abraham carried many of these qualities of a friend: he was faithful; he was a peacemaker; he pursued justice rather than using his relationships to acquire more stuff; he was obedient to the terms of the covenant he made with God.

We looked at a visit from God, who told Abraham and Sarah that finally their waiting was over. The son of the covenant, whom God had promised, would be born within the year. We see everything the Lord, Abraham's three visitors, spoke about, came to be even the destruction of the arrogant and selfish communities of Sodom and Gomorrah.

I once had a dream that I was pregnant... and I was so anticipating the joy of being a mother. But in the dream, when the baby was born, it was severely disabled. It was so mal formed, that it was grotesque to look at; the health problems were constant and overwhelming.... The devastation of this reality was difficult. My reality looked nothing like the dream.
At that time, I had no difficulty drawing the parallel between this dream and my experience of being a pastor. Something I had loved and nurtured and held as closely as a pregnant mother, wanting to be part of. When it was actually born it didn't look like or feel like what I anticipated at all. In fact, it felt grotesque and overwhelming.
I was talking with a Spiritual Director about this dream, and she said to me, "Why don't you let this baby die? It seems that in some cultures they

will take malformed babies outside, abandon them, and allow them to die."

And I thought about that the idea of laying this dream down at the cross and exposing it to death, and how that could even be considered a spiritual thing. It was then I realised something. The dream still had life. It wasn't dead yet. This dream, with all of its problems, still had life. If a child has life... then as a mother, I am mandated to protect it. So the only way for me to understand this dream was that my sacrifice was not to abandon it, or kill it, but to offer myself as a living sacrifice and care for it, with all of its problems, and trust that in some way God would resurrect it, restore it, heal it... to the first anticipated intention.

As we conclude our journey with Abraham... we are looking at how he has been holding something in his heart that is anticipated, but it is not as simple and as beautiful as they had dreamed.

Bible Reading
Genesis 21:1-7

Isaac – 'one who rejoices'
The laughter that was mocking before, has turned to joy and wonder. Their son is named Isaac – "one who laughs; one who rejoices". Isaac is circumcised on the eighth day. This is the child of covenant, and the terms of their covenant are remembered. Even with this blessing, all is not happy in the tents of Abraham.

Bible Reading
Genesis 21:8-13

Ishmael turns to mocking

Ishmael is a youth now. He has been the focus of his Father's attention his entire life. Now suddenly there is another son, another object of his father's affection. A son who Abraham will throw a feast for... for the simple reason he is weaned. A child is transitioning from the nursery to the schoolroom of men. Ancient times – ancient story. We are not talking about a one-year-old or a two-year-old. Isaac may have been 5 or 6 years old when he was weaned.

It is not so surprising that Ishmael resists the change; he pushes back. He lashes out and bullies Isaac, mocks him. Not surprising. God told Hagar her son would be a wild donkey, against all his brothers.

Inheritance safeguarded

If you are ever brave enough to have a go at someone's kids, you can expect a parent to activate 'protective mode'. Sarah is outraged. She demands Ishmael be disinherited... disowned... renounced. She is very clear: she now considers Ishmael, illegitimate... the son of a slave. She moves to not just protect her son from a bully, but his inheritance.

How does Abraham manage this? Because this involves both his sons. He goes to God for wisdom in his distress. Did you notice God doesn't say, "If you had listened to me in the first place you wouldn't be in this mess?"
Or: "There are always consequences when you don't follow through, and now you have to manage this fallout yourself?"
Or: "You made your bed, (literally with the slave girl) and now you have to lie in it."

I think it is very easy to overlay the kind of wisdom that we dish out over the BBQ or around the water-cooler and then transfer that stance onto God's character. Yes, all of those observations have an element of truth:

Abraham did move prematurely... he didn't wait. This was a mess. He contributed to the mess. But God never abandons his friend to work out how to do the best manage the consequences of the mess alone.

When Jesus said, "I am with you always..." He is quoting the words of God that we find in Old Testament... three times...

Bible References
Deuteronomy 31:6; Joshua 1:5; 1 Chronicles 28:20.

Jesus is the manifest wisdom of God and his nature. God will never leave us nor forsake us. He is with us always, even when... He will help us sort through the maze of problems, if our heart is to include God.

In this situation, God allows Abraham to have Hagar and Ishmael leave home as Sarah demanded. Ishmael was probably 18 or 19 years of age that this stage. I've had this picture in my mind that Abraham was abandoning a child of nine or ten.

Ishmael is a young man now, and together with his mother, they can make their way. Things have changed from when Hagar was pregnant and alone. God will still keep his promises that there is a blessing over Ishmael life as Abraham's son.

God intervenes

But the reality is, that move was hard on Hagar and Ishmael. They get a long way, but then they become stuck in the in-between. Between where they have come from and where they were going, finding a home that is their own. Isn't it encouraging that God will intervene where we have no control?

God intervenes for Hagar and Ishmael and sends angels to minister to them. He shows them the provision of water. They are strengthened.

They establish a place of their own to call home. Ishmael develops skills as an outstanding archer. Hagar provides Ishmael with a wife from her own people, an Egyptian. Ishmael has twelve sons. God's promise is that he would become a great nation in his own right.

Later on, we read in Genesis that the Ishmaelites have become renown and influential traders between their land and Egypt. The brothers of Joseph sold him to an Ishmaelites caravan of traders who were on their trade-route to Egypt. We see in the long view, that God protected Hagar and Ishmael. They found a new normal.

Life in Abraham's tents also resumes. Isaac becomes the only son, the heir of his father's household. And then something happens that again challenges this re-established equilibrium.

Bible Reading
Genesis 22:1-8

Deep devotion
This is another one of those stories that is difficult to get our head around. The account says that God was testing Abraham. One way to understand these types of divine tests is as an *opportunity*. An opportunity to show our deep devotion to God.

Unfortunately, this same opportunity can be taken and twisted by Satan into a devious trap that is intended to harm us. So why would God test Abraham's devotion in this way? Why would he ask Abraham to sacrifice of his son?

Remember... Ancient times, ancient story.

Right at the beginning of this journey we looked at Abraham's background. He grew up surrounded by his father's idols, and the culture and worship of the nations around them – particularly Chemosh and Molech. We talked about how the worship of these gods regularly required their devotion to be demonstrated in extreme and sadistic ways. The god Molech was one of the deities worshiped at this time by the people of Sodom and Gomorrah before it was destroyed. Archaeological excavations[v] of places where there was worship offered to the god Molech, have unearthed hundreds of ancient urns containing the charred bones of children, who were offered as sacrificial gifts to this god. In ancient times, this was a standard understanding of how devotion and deep worship to a god was practiced.

As we read on, we understand that God does not require this kind of sacrifice to demonstrate deep devotion. It says this directive is a test. God is checking his heart... testing his devotion. But perhaps God is starting with the cultural understanding of what it means to be completely devoted... deep worship... and then taking Abraham to a place that is more aligned with how he desires his relationship with people to be. God is moving Abraham into a deeper awareness of who God is.

When we hear this instruction: "Sacrifice your son as a burnt offering" we are horrified, we recoil, and we want to throw up. Ancient times; ancient story.

When Abraham heard this directive, it was not unusual; it is likely he would have thought... "Oh. Well, okay then." This is what he grew up with. This is what he witnessed around him in the frenzied worship of idols. His devotion to God was costly. This costly. Sacrifice was the price of deep worship. He understood this was an opportunity to demonstrate his profound devotion to God.

Demonstrated obedience

Did Abraham want to this? No. Of course not. Everything within him most likely resisted this. But he trusted God. He trusted in the God El Elyon – El Elyon, the Lord of Heaven and Earth, whom the priest Melchizedek worshipped.

Abraham didn't question whether this was the word of God. He is familiar now with the God who speaks, he knew his voice. He knew it was the word of God. He didn't argue the truth of what God asked. He knew what he had to do. But he did it with an understanding of the promises of God. He was able to obey because he had a profound confidence in the God who caused them as a couple to conceive in old age is the same God who could do whatever was needed to see his promises come to pass.

Trust in divine provision

It doesn't say how old Isaac was when this directive was given. Most artistic depictions have him as a boy, barely 10 years old. Some Jewish commentaries have him as old as 37. It appears likely he was a young man, 16-20 years old. So... we have a strong young man and an old man, over 100 years old. Although Abraham is still able to climb mountains, if Isaac wanted to resist, it is expected that he could have easily overcome his elderly father and headed for the hills.

This account talks about Abraham's heart devotion... but I think it equally makes a comment about Isaac's heart. Abraham's heart trusted his Father-God. Isaac's heart trusted his father who loved him. It seems to me that this sacrifice is consensual. The son is in complete agreeance and in obedience to the father. So perhaps the binding of Isaac, was not to stop his struggling to get away. Perhaps it was done with mutual consent so that Isaac himself could also follow through on what Abraham was required to do.

Abraham speaks out the confidence that God will provide a lamb for the sacrifice. All he knows is that from what God has said, the lamb for this sacrifice is to be his son. He has no understanding of a Plan B. But he expects God to make this right. If God requires a sacrifice, and the promise dies, then God would also provide a resurrection to make the promise be fulfilled. God could do that. In Hebrews, this is what we are told:

Bible Reading
Hebrews 11:17-19

They reached the place... Mt Moriah
Abraham and Isaac set out and reach the place where God had directed them to go... to Mount Moriah. This was intentional destination. A destination that God has designated as significant.

Bible Reading
Genesis 22: 9-19

We have seen Mt Moriah before when we were looking at the life of David. It was on Mt Moriah that David bought the threshing floor from Araunah the Jebusite – a farmer from Jerusalem. It was here on Mt Moriah that David built an altar to God, to atone for his sin in conducting the census, so that the sickness that was plaguing the people would be stopped. David sacrificed there and God accepted his worship by sending fire from Heaven to consume the sacrifice.

Bible Reference
1 Chronicles 21:25-26

It was on this same place on Mt Moriah that Solomon built the temple of the Lord.

Bible Reference
2 Chronicles 3:1

This is the place where Abraham and Isaac came to meet with God This was the place God designated for them to offer a demonstration of their deep devotion. First and foremost, this coming to Mt Moriah was an act of worship. One rending of the word Moriah... is that it is play on words... "the land of Myrrh". Myrrh and spices were used in fragrant worship.

Is my worship like the fragrant incense of Myrrh?

Mt Moriah is the place where God was to be worshipped in awesome wonder. The temple was to stand on this site, where incense and myrrh would be burnt in beautiful aroma of worship.

Bible Reference
Psalm 141:2

Mt Moriah is the place where Abraham and Isaac came to worship. There is another idea that the Mountain Moriah had the meaning "the land of teaching", so the name Moriah is also connected to the idea of instruction... learning and being taught.

Yes, there was so much for Abraham, even over 100 years of age, was to learn about his friendship and relationship with God. Down the years, the temple was to become a place of learning about what it meant to walk in the ways of God. This is the place where Abraham and Isaac came to learn of God, from God.

How open am I to the idea of learning more about God, and his Word, or do I prefer the simplicity of new-Christian immature faith?

God is the Main thing

The beautiful thing about this act of worship is that it shows where Abraham's priorities lie. God is number one. The main thing stays the main thing. The main thing for Abraham is his relationship with God.

Abraham doesn't get so caught up in the promise of having a family, or a legacy, or fame, or making a difference... that these ideas became more important than God who was gifting these things to him. These are all positive things... but Abraham never forgot about the why... and his "why" was his friendship with God. God was the reason these other things would be added.

Is the main thing... still the main thing in my life?
Where has that got a little out of whack?

Jesus said it so beautifully...

Bibe Reference
Matthew 6:33

Abraham was willing to let all that die... and prioritised God over everything else. God acknowledges this... "I know that you fear God, because you have not withheld from me your son, your only son." He was willing to lay down the thing that he held dearest to his heart, because God had the priority place of being first. What we find is that because he kept this order of things, it opened the door for God to do all the other stuff as well. Abundantly... but even if he didn't... God still was first.

A map of salvation

This interaction on Mt Moriah also becomes a map of salvation that God is recording for his people down through the generations. Mt Moriah is a place of worship, a place of learning.

Abraham and Isaac build an altar there to worship God in obedience. King David, fourteen generations later – builds an altar on Mt Moriah to atone for his disobedience and to intercede for the people if Israel. King Solomon, builds the magnificent temple there, a beautiful and fragrant place of worship, atonement and learning.

It is here, as Isaac allows himself to be bound, and lays on the altar in sacrifice... that God changes everything!

"Abraham!" God says. He calls him by name. "Abraham! Don't lay a hand on your only son. I know you are devoted in your heart."

Then Abraham sees what he had not seen before but had been there all along. He saw the provision of the sacrificial lamb that he believed that God would provide. God provided the sacrificial lamb. There, in the thicket, was a ram tangled up by the horns.

Abraham calls out a new revelation of the name of God: 'Jehovah Jireh'... the God who provides! God provided a way to worship – without human sacrifice being needed to demonstrate our devotion. God provided a way to worship – a pathway of redemption that offers life, not death. God provided a way to worship – the fragrance of our obedience and faithfulness, like the incense of Myrrh, rising up to be an acceptable offering before the Lord. God provided a way to worship – giving us what we need, so we can offer it back to him as an expression of our devotion.

When we call on the name Jehovah Jireh, we are calling on the God who provides. This provision, however, is from God who facilitates our worship, not our indulgence. If we use the name Jehovah Jireh to perpetuate a prosperity-doctrine of indulgence, I wonder if we are using his name to sign cheques that God did not authorise and using his name in vain?

Jehovah Jireh provided everything Abraham and Isaac needed to worship him more fully. Can you imagine... how Abraham and Isaac felt after seeing the hand of the Lord reach out to intervene in this way, teaching them, that human sacrifice is now off the altar forever. Jehovah Jireh would provide an acceptable way of worship that offers life... a fuller, fulfilling life, an abundant life! Can you imagine how their worship would have gone from deep to deeper!

Are there things that I need God – Jehovah Jireh, to provide in my life?

Praise be to God Almighty! What was, and is, and is to come! We have seen how Abraham became, in so many matters, the forerunner... the precedent, of the Law. Human sacrifice, as a form of worship was now to be written into the Law of Moses as something that God found repugnant.

Bible Reference
Deuteronomy 18:9-10

It wasn't that God suddenly had a revelation that this wasn't a good idea... after all it was God who suggested this trip up the mountain. This was, as we say, 'a teaching moment', on the mountain of teaching. From now on, it was unambiguous and clear. Animal sacrifice is enough.

God gives a fresh revelation in the New Covenant, that even animal sacrifices have become obsolete. Jesus' sacrifice is enough. Our faithful, faith-filled worship is enough.

Final thoughts...
God visits Abraham and asks him to sacrifice his son Isaac on a mountain called Moriah. It is a meeting place of worship. Abraham goes there to demonstrate his deep devotion for God. However, God intervenes, and delivers them another sacrifice, an animal instead.

In a profound way, God is showing Abraham a map of his salvation, as God who provides the sacrificial lamb. He paves the way for more understanding of how God provides for his people as Jehovah Jireh.

I remember the first time I had a short article published in a magazine. It was thrilling. I was so excited that I danced around the kitchen. I had no concept that life could be better than this! But at one point, I came to the realisation that my writing was not to be anything more than just a pleasure, a hobby I had for myself... a private thing. I was a laying it down. Years later I have many fiction titles published... including children's books... and these Bible Reflection books. What I had laid down, God resurrected... and made alive and multiplied!

Paul writes to the Romans this insight:

Bible Reference
Romans 12:1

It is not that sacrifice is no longer needed... but the form of sacrifice has changed. God doesn't require us to physically die to be a sacrifice, but we are to be living sacrifices.
Living a life that dies to our own agendas.
Living a life that worships God in everything that we do.
Living a life that is open to learning more about God and his way.
Living a life that is a peacemaker.
Living a life that doesn't perpetuate corruption but pursues justice.
Living a life that is kind and merciful.
Living a life that is generous and open handed to the poor and needy.
Living a life that is obedient to God's choices.
Living a life that acts justly... and loves mercy... and walks humbly with our God.

Of the friendship qualities of Abraham...
    Being a peacemaker...
    Pursuing justice...
    Being obedient
    Having a merciful heart
    Being faithful
Which of these qualities am I solid in?
Which of these qualities do I need to grow?

By living like this... loving each other... we love God in a profound way, and I think this summarises the qualities that made Abraham a friend of God.

Prayer:

Father God, it is humbling to know, Jehovah Jireh that you provide everything that we need to worship you more fully. Thank you that you have given us things in our hand so that we can offer it back to you as an acceptable offering. Thank you that you do desire our deep worship as living sacrifices. Father, thank you that you have not relegated these qualities of friendship to the great patriarchs of old, but by your Holy Spirit that you would empower and equip us today, to be the best friend we can be... to act justly, love mercy, and walk humbly before you...
In Jesus Name, Amen.

Other books in this Series

Endnotes

i Molech: A God of Human Sacrifice in the Old Testament. John Day.
This article was published in The Biblical Archaeologist (1938-1997), which is continued by Near Eastern Archaeology (1998-present). Copyright 1992 American Schools of Oriental Research

ii "Is not this written in the Book of Jasher?" (Joshua, 10:13).
"Behold it is written in the Book of Jasher." (II Samuel 1:18)
"Accounts in the Bible can be made more lucid and easier to understand with the background of "The Book of Jasher" in mind."
[Faithfully translated (1840) from the Original Hebrew into English. A Reprint of Photo Lithographic Reprint of Exact Edition Published by J.H. Parry & Co. 1887]

iii. Study by the Cultural Research Centre of Arizona Christian University
Dr. George Barna, "American Worldview Inventory 2021: Release #6," Arizona Christian University Cultural Research Center (August 31, 2021),
https://www.arizonachristian.edu/wp-content/uploads/2021/08/CRC_AWVI2021_Release06_Digital_01_20210831.pdf
.

iv Elisabeth Taylor, 2018, "Pornography as a Public Health Issue: Promoting Violence and Exploitation of Children, Youth, and Adults.", Centre for Human Dignity'

v Molech: A God of Human Sacrifice in the Old Testament. John Day.
This article was published in The Biblical Archaeologist (1938-1997), which is continued by Near Eastern Archaeology(1998-present). Copyright 1992 American Schools of Oriental Research

www.ingramcontent.com/pod-product-compliance
Lightning Source LLC
Chambersburg PA
CBHW052107070526
44584CB00017B/2375